Introducing our Mediterranean Recipes Cookbook, a celebration of the vibrant and flavorful cuisine that is beloved all around the Mediterranean Sea.

This cookbook is packed with over 50 recipes that are inspired by the traditional dishes of countries such as Italy, Greece, Spain, and Turkey, as well as the Middle East and North Africa. Each recipe showcases the fresh and colorful ingredients that are characteristic of Mediterranean cooking, such as juicy tomatoes, fragrant herbs, and tangy citrus fruits.

Whether you're a seasoned cook or just starting out in the kitchen, this cookbook is perfect for anyone who loves to cook and eat delicious, healthy food. From comforting stews and savory meat dishes, to refreshing salads and hearty vegetarian options, there is something for everyone in this collection of recipes.

Our cookbook includes easy-to-follow instructions, beautiful photographs, and helpful tips for sourcing ingredients and making substitutions. It also features a comprehensive introduction to Mediterranean cooking, including the history and cultural significance of the cuisine.

With our Mediterranean Recipes Cookbook, you can bring the flavors of the Mediterranean into your home and create delicious and healthy meals that your family and friends will love. So whether you're looking to expand your culinary horizons or simply enjoy a delicious meal, this cookbook is the perfect choice for you.

Gambas al Ajillo

Ingredients:

1 pound of raw shrimp, peeled and deveined
6 cloves of garlic, sliced thinly
1/4 cup of olive oil
1/2 teaspoon of red pepper flakes
1 tablespoon of freshly squeezed lemon juice
Salt and pepper, to taste
Fresh parsley, chopped (optional)

Instructions:

Heat olive oil in a large skillet over medium-high heat.
Add sliced garlic and red pepper flakes to the skillet, stirring frequently until garlic is fragrant and lightly browned, about 2-3 minutes.
Add the shrimp to the skillet, season with salt and pepper, and stir to coat with the garlic oil.
Cook the shrimp for 3-4 minutes on each side, until they are pink and cooked through.
Squeeze lemon juice over the shrimp and stir to combine.
Remove the skillet from heat, garnish with chopped parsley, and serve immediately.
Enjoy your Gambas al Ajillo with crusty bread or over a bed of rice!

Harissa Shrimp

Ingredients:

1 pound of large raw shrimp, peeled and deveined
2-3 tablespoons of harissa paste (depending on your spice preference)
1/4 cup of olive oil
2 garlic cloves, minced
1/2 teaspoon of ground cumin
1/2 teaspoon of paprika
Salt and pepper, to taste
Lemon wedges and chopped parsley, for serving (optional)

Instructions:

In a small bowl, mix together the harissa paste, olive oil, minced garlic, ground cumin, and paprika.
Season the shrimp with salt and pepper, and toss them in the harissa mixture until they are coated evenly.
Cover the bowl with plastic wrap and refrigerate for at least 30 minutes to marinate.
Heat a large skillet over medium-high heat.
Add the shrimp to the skillet and cook for about 2-3 minutes on each side, or until they are pink and cooked through.
Serve the shrimp immediately, garnished with lemon wedges and chopped parsley if desired.
Enjoy your spicy and flavorful Harissa Shrimp with a side salad or your favorite Mediterranean side dishes!

Mediterranean Fish with Tapenade

Ingredients:

4 (6-ounce) fish fillets (such as sea bass or halibut)
Salt and pepper, to taste
2 tablespoons of olive oil
1/4 cup of black olive tapenade
1/4 cup of chopped fresh parsley
2 garlic cloves, minced
2 tablespoons of freshly squeezed lemon juice
Lemon wedges, for serving

Instructions:

Preheat your oven to 400°F.
Season the fish fillets with salt and pepper on both sides.
Heat olive oil in an oven-proof skillet over medium-high heat.
Sear the fish fillets in the skillet for about 2 minutes on each side until golden brown.
In a small bowl, mix together the tapenade, chopped parsley, minced garlic, and lemon juice.
Spread the tapenade mixture over the tops of the fish fillets.
Transfer the skillet to the oven and bake for 8-10 minutes, or until the fish is cooked through and the tapenade is hot and bubbly.
Serve the fish fillets immediately, garnished with lemon wedges.
Enjoy your delicious Mediterranean Fish with Tapenade with a side of roasted vegetables or a simple green salad.

Clam Linguine (Linguine alle Vongole)

Ingredients:

1 pound linguine
2 tablespoons of olive oil
4 garlic cloves, minced
1/2 teaspoon of red pepper flakes (optional)
1/2 cup of dry white wine
2 pounds of fresh clams, scrubbed
1/4 cup of chopped fresh parsley
Salt and pepper, to taste
Lemon wedges, for serving

Instructions:

Cook the linguine according to package instructions until al dente.
Meanwhile, heat olive oil in a large skillet over medium heat.
Add the minced garlic and red pepper flakes (if using) to the skillet, stirring frequently until garlic is fragrant and lightly browned, about 2-3 minutes.
Pour in the white wine and bring it to a simmer.
Add the clams to the skillet and cover with a lid.
Cook the clams for about 5-7 minutes or until they have opened, discarding any clams that haven't opened.
Drain the linguine and add it to the skillet with the clams and sauce.
Add chopped parsley and season with salt and pepper to taste.
Toss everything together until the linguine is coated with the sauce.
Serve the Clam Linguine immediately, garnished with lemon wedges.
Enjoy your flavorful Mediterranean Clam Linguine with a glass of white wine and some crusty bread to soak up the delicious sauce.

Shakshuka

Ingredients:

1 large onion, chopped
2 bell peppers (red, yellow, or green), seeded and chopped
4 garlic cloves, minced
1 teaspoon of ground cumin
1 teaspoon of smoked paprika
1/4 teaspoon of cayenne pepper (optional)
1 (28-ounce) can of whole peeled tomatoes, crushed by hand
1/2 cup of vegetable or chicken broth
6-8 large eggs
Salt and pepper, to taste
Fresh parsley or cilantro, chopped, for serving (optional)

Instructions:

Heat olive oil in a large skillet over medium heat.
Add the chopped onion and bell peppers to the skillet, and cook for about 5-7 minutes until softened.
Add minced garlic, ground cumin, smoked paprika, and cayenne pepper (if using) to the skillet, stirring frequently for another 1-2 minutes until fragrant.
Add the crushed tomatoes and vegetable or chicken broth to the skillet, season with salt and pepper to taste, and bring the mixture to a simmer.
Simmer the sauce for about 10-15 minutes until it has thickened and reduced slightly.
Using a spoon, create 6-8 wells in the sauce.
Crack an egg into each well and season the eggs with salt and pepper.
Cover the skillet and cook on medium-low heat for about 5-10 minutes or until the eggs are set to your desired consistency.
Remove the skillet from heat and sprinkle with fresh parsley or cilantro if desired.
Serve the Shakshuka hot with some crusty bread or pita bread to soak up the delicious sauce.
Enjoy your flavorful Mediterranean Shakshuka as a brunch or dinner dish!

Espinacas con Garbanzos

Ingredients:

2 cans of chickpeas (15 ounces each), drained and rinsed
1/4 cup of olive oil
4 garlic cloves, minced
1 onion, chopped
1 teaspoon of ground cumin
1 teaspoon of smoked paprika
1/2 teaspoon of ground coriander
1/4 teaspoon of cayenne pepper (optional)
1 (14-ounce) can of diced tomatoes, drained
1/2 cup of water or vegetable broth
Salt and pepper, to taste
1 pound of fresh spinach, washed and trimmed
Lemon wedges, for serving

Instructions:

Heat the olive oil in a large skillet over medium heat.
Add the minced garlic and chopped onion to the skillet, stirring frequently until fragrant and lightly browned, about 2-3 minutes.
Add the ground cumin, smoked paprika, ground coriander, and cayenne pepper (if using), and cook for another 1-2 minutes until fragrant.
Add the drained chickpeas to the skillet and stir to coat with the spice mixture.
Pour in the diced tomatoes and water or vegetable broth to the skillet, season with salt and pepper to taste, and bring the mixture to a simmer.
Simmer the chickpeas for about 10-15 minutes until the sauce has thickened slightly.
Add the fresh spinach to the skillet in batches, stirring until the spinach has wilted and is fully incorporated into the sauce.
Cook for an additional 2-3 minutes until the spinach is cooked through.
Remove the skillet from heat and serve the Espinacas con Garbanzos hot, garnished with lemon wedges.
Enjoy your delicious Espinacas con Garbanzos as a vegetarian main dish or as a side dish with grilled meat or fish.

Olive Tapenade

Ingredients:

1 1/2 cups of pitted Kalamata olives
2 garlic cloves, minced
2 tablespoons of capers, drained and rinsed
1 tablespoon of fresh lemon juice
1 tablespoon of Dijon mustard
1/4 cup of fresh parsley leaves, chopped
1/4 cup of fresh basil leaves, chopped
1/4 cup of extra-virgin olive oil
Salt and pepper, to taste

Instructions:

Place the pitted Kalamata olives, minced garlic, and capers in a food processor and pulse until coarsely chopped.
Add the fresh lemon juice, Dijon mustard, chopped parsley and basil leaves, and pulse again until the mixture is finely chopped.
With the food processor running, slowly pour in the extra-virgin olive oil through the feed tube until the mixture is well combined and has a smooth consistency.
Season the olive tapenade with salt and pepper to taste.
Transfer the olive tapenade to a bowl and refrigerate for at least 30 minutes to allow the flavors to meld together.
Serve the olive tapenade cold, garnished with additional chopped herbs or drizzled with more olive oil, if desired.
Enjoy your delicious and flavorful Mediterranean olive tapenade as a snack or as a condiment to elevate your dishes!

Chicken Cacciatore

Here's a recipe for a classic Mediterranean chicken cacciatore, a hearty and flavorful dish that combines chicken, vegetables, and herbs in a delicious tomato-based sauce:

Ingredients:

4 chicken thighs
4 chicken drumsticks
Salt and pepper, to taste
2 tablespoons of olive oil
1 onion, chopped
3 garlic cloves, minced
1 red bell pepper, seeded and sliced
1 yellow bell pepper, seeded and sliced
1 (14-ounce) can of diced tomatoes
1/2 cup of chicken broth
1/4 cup of red wine (optional)
1 tablespoon of tomato paste
1 tablespoon of dried oregano
1 tablespoon of dried basil
1 bay leaf
1/2 cup of pitted Kalamata olives
2 tablespoons of capers, drained and rinsed
Fresh parsley, chopped, for garnish

Instructions:

Season the chicken thighs and drumsticks with salt and pepper.

Heat the olive oil in a large Dutch oven or heavy-bottomed pot over medium-high heat.

Add the chicken pieces to the pot and brown them on all sides, about 5-7 minutes per side.
Remove the chicken from the pot and set it aside.
Add the chopped onion, minced garlic, and sliced bell peppers to the pot and sauté them until softened, about 5-7 minutes.
Add the diced tomatoes, chicken broth, red wine (if using), tomato paste, dried oregano, dried basil, and bay leaf to the pot and stir to combine.
Return the chicken pieces to the pot and spoon the sauce over them.
Bring the mixture to a simmer, reduce the heat to low, cover the pot, and cook for about 30-40 minutes until the chicken is tender and cooked through.
Add the pitted Kalamata olives and capers to the pot and stir to combine.
Cook for an additional 5-10 minutes until the sauce has thickened slightly.
Remove the bay leaf from the pot and discard it.
Serve the chicken cacciatore hot, garnished with chopped fresh parsley.
Enjoy your delicious and comforting Mediterranean chicken cacciatore with a side of crusty bread or over pasta!

Tzatziki

Tzatziki is a delicious and refreshing Greek dip made with yogurt, cucumber, garlic, and fresh herbs. Here's a simple recipe to make it at home:

Ingredients:

1 cup of Greek yogurt
1/2 cup of grated cucumber
1-2 garlic cloves, minced
1 tablespoon of fresh lemon juice
1 tablespoon of extra-virgin olive oil
1 tablespoon of chopped fresh dill
Salt and pepper, to taste

Instructions:

Place the Greek yogurt in a mixing bowl and stir until it is smooth and creamy.
Add the grated cucumber, minced garlic, fresh lemon juice, extra-virgin olive oil, and chopped fresh dill to the bowl.
Season the mixture with salt and pepper to taste and stir well to combine all the ingredients.
Cover the bowl and refrigerate the tzatziki for at least 30 minutes to allow the flavors to meld together.
Before serving, give the tzatziki a quick stir and adjust the seasoning if needed.
Serve the tzatziki cold as a dip with pita bread, vegetables, or grilled meats.
Enjoy your delicious and healthy Mediterranean tzatziki dip as a snack or appetizer!

Caponata – Sicilian Eggplant Relish

Caponata is a Sicilian dish made with eggplant, tomatoes, onions, and celery, seasoned with capers, olives, and vinegar. It can be served as a relish or a side dish, and it is delicious on bread or with grilled meats. Here's a recipe to make it at home:

Ingredients:

2 large eggplants, diced into 1-inch pieces
Salt, for sprinkling
1/4 cup of olive oil
1 onion, chopped
2 celery stalks, chopped
1 red bell pepper, seeded and chopped
3 garlic cloves, minced
1 (14-ounce) can of diced tomatoes, drained
1/4 cup of red wine vinegar
1/4 cup of sugar
1/2 cup of pitted green olives, chopped
1/4 cup of capers, drained and rinsed
1/4 cup of chopped fresh parsley
Salt and pepper, to taste

Instructions:

Place the diced eggplant in a colander and sprinkle it with salt. Toss the eggplant to coat it evenly with the salt and let it sit for about 30 minutes to release excess moisture.
Rinse the eggplant under running water and pat it dry with paper towels.

Heat the olive oil in a large skillet over medium heat.

Add the chopped onion, chopped celery, and chopped red bell pepper to the skillet and sauté them until they are softened, about 5-7 minutes.
Add the minced garlic to the skillet and sauté for another minute until fragrant.
Add the diced eggplant to the skillet and sauté it until it is softened and golden brown, about 10-15 minutes.
Add the drained diced tomatoes, red wine vinegar, and sugar to the skillet and stir well to combine.
Reduce the heat to low, cover the skillet, and simmer the caponata for about 30 minutes until it is thick and flavorful.
Stir in the chopped green olives, drained capers, and chopped fresh parsley.
Season the caponata with salt and pepper to taste.
Remove the skillet from the heat and let the caponata cool to room temperature.
Serve the caponata as a relish or a side dish, garnished with additional chopped parsley if desired.
Enjoy your delicious and flavorful Mediterranean caponata as a side dish or appetizer!

Moutabal

Moutabal is a delicious Middle Eastern dip made with grilled eggplant, tahini, garlic, and lemon juice. It is similar to baba ghanoush, but with a creamier texture and a nuttier flavor. Here's a recipe to make it at home:

Ingredients:

2 medium eggplants
2 garlic cloves, minced
2 tablespoons of tahini
2 tablespoons of fresh lemon juice
1/4 cup of extra-virgin olive oil
Salt and pepper, to taste
Chopped fresh parsley, for garnish

Instructions:

Preheat the oven to 400°F.
Prick the eggplants all over with a fork and place them on a baking sheet lined with parchment paper.
Roast the eggplants in the oven for about 45 minutes, until they are soft and collapsed.
Remove the eggplants from the oven and let them cool for about 10 minutes.
Cut the eggplants in half lengthwise and scoop out the flesh into a bowl.
Mash the eggplant flesh with a fork or a potato masher until it is smooth and creamy.
Add the minced garlic, tahini, fresh lemon juice, and extra-virgin olive oil to the bowl.
Season the moutabal with salt and pepper to taste and stir well to combine all the ingredients.
Cover the bowl and refrigerate the moutabal for at least 30 minutes to allow the flavors to meld together.
Before serving, give the moutabal a quick stir and adjust the seasoning if needed.
Serve the moutabal cold as a dip with pita bread, vegetables, or grilled meats, garnished with chopped fresh parsley.
Enjoy your delicious and healthy Mediterranean moutabal dip as a snack or appetizer!

Hummus

Hummus is a delicious and healthy dip made from chickpeas, tahini, lemon juice, garlic, and olive oil. Here is a recipe for Mediterranean-style hummus:

Ingredients:

2 cans of chickpeas, drained and rinsed
1/4 cup tahini
1/4 cup fresh lemon juice
2 cloves garlic, minced
1/2 teaspoon ground cumin
Salt to taste
1/4 cup extra-virgin olive oil, plus more for drizzling
Optional toppings: chopped parsley, paprika, pine nuts

Instructions:

In a food processor or blender, combine the chickpeas, tahini, lemon juice, garlic, cumin, and salt. Pulse until well combined.
With the motor running, slowly drizzle in the olive oil until the hummus is smooth and creamy. If the hummus is too thick, add a tablespoon of water at a time until you reach your desired consistency.
Taste and adjust seasoning as needed, adding more salt or lemon juice to taste.
To serve, transfer the hummus to a serving bowl and drizzle with olive oil. Garnish with chopped parsley, paprika, and pine nuts if desired.
Serve with pita bread, sliced vegetales, or crackers for dipping. Enjoy your delicious Mediterranean-style hummus!

Fasolada

Fasolada is a traditional Mediterranean soup made with white beans, vegetables, and herbs. Here is a recipe for Fasolada:

Ingredients:

2 cups dried white beans, soaked overnight
1 large onion, chopped
2-3 garlic cloves, minced
2 carrots, peeled and chopped
2 celery stalks, chopped
1 can of diced tomatoes
1/4 cup olive oil
1 tablespoon tomato paste
1 tablespoon dried oregano
2 bay leaves
4 cups vegetable broth or water
Salt and pepper to taste
Lemon wedges and fresh parsley for serving

Instructions:

Rinse the soaked white beans and place them in a large pot with enough water to cover them by about an inch. Bring the pot to a boil and cook the beans until they are tender, about 45 minutes to an hour.
While the beans are cooking, heat the olive oil in a large pot over medium heat. Add the chopped onion and garlic, and sauté until the onion is soft and translucent, about 5-7 minutes.
Add the chopped carrots and celery to the pot, and sauté for an additional 5 minutes.
Add the diced tomatoes, tomato paste, oregano, bay leaves, and vegetable broth or water to the pot. Bring the mixture to a boil, then reduce the heat to low and let it simmer for 15-20 minutes.
Once the white beans are cooked, drain them and add them to the pot with the vegetables and broth. Stir everything together and let the soup simmer for another 10-15 minutes, until the vegetables are tender and the flavors have melded together.
Taste the soup and add salt and pepper as needed.
Serve the Fasolada hot, garnished with fresh parsley and a wedge of lemon to squeeze over the top. Enjoy your delicious and nutritious Mediterranean soup!

Beef Tagine (Moroccan Beef Stew)

Ingredients:

2 lbs beef chuck, cut into 1-inch cubes
1 large onion, chopped
3 garlic cloves, minced
1 tablespoon fresh ginger, grated
2 teaspoons paprika
2 teaspoons ground cumin
1/2 teaspoon ground cinnamon
1/2 teaspoon ground coriander
1/4 teaspoon ground cardamom
1/4 teaspoon cayenne pepper
1 teaspoon salt
1/2 teaspoon black pepper
2 tablespoons olive oil
2 cups beef broth
1 cup canned diced tomatoes, undrained
1 cup pitted dates, chopped
1/4 cup fresh cilantro, chopped
1/4 cup fresh parsley, chopped
1/4 cup slivered almonds, toasted

Instructions:

In a large pot or dutch oven, heat the olive oil over medium-high heat. Add the onions and sauté for 2-3 minutes, until softened. Add the garlic and ginger and cook for another minute.

Add the beef cubes to the pot and cook for 5-7 minutes, until browned on all sides.

Add the paprika, cumin, cinnamon, coriander, cardamom, cayenne pepper, salt, and black pepper to the pot. Stir to coat the beef evenly with the spices.

Pour in the beef broth and diced tomatoes. Bring the mixture to a boil, then reduce the heat to low and simmer for 1-2 hours, until the beef is tender.

Add the chopped dates to the pot and stir to combine. Cook for another 10-15 minutes, until the dates are softened and the stew has thickened.

Garnish the stew with chopped cilantro, parsley, and slivered almonds before serving.

Serve the beef tagine with rice or couscous, and enjoy!

Spanish Clams with Chorizo

Ingredients:

1 lb fresh clams, scrubbed and rinsed
2 tablespoons olive oil
2 oz chorizo, sliced
1 small onion, chopped
2 garlic cloves, minced
1/2 teaspoon smoked paprika
1/4 teaspoon cayenne pepper
1/2 cup dry white wine
2 tablespoons chopped fresh parsley
Salt and pepper to taste
Lemon wedges, for serving

Instructions:

In a large skillet, heat the olive oil over medium heat. Add the sliced chorizo and cook for 2-3 minutes, until browned and crispy. Remove the chorizo from the skillet and set aside.
Add the chopped onion to the skillet and cook for 2-3 minutes, until softened. Add the minced garlic, smoked paprika, and cayenne pepper, and cook for another minute.
Pour in the white wine and bring the mixture to a simmer. Add the clams to the skillet and cover with a lid. Cook for 3-4 minutes, shaking the skillet occasionally, until the clams have opened.
Discard any clams that have not opened. Return the chorizo to the skillet and stir to combine with the clams and sauce.
Season the dish with salt and pepper to taste. Garnish with chopped fresh parsley and serve with lemon wedges on the side.
Enjoy your Spanish Clams with Chorizo with some crusty bread to soak up the delicious sauce!

Moroccan Lentil Soup

Ingredients:

2 tablespoons olive oil
1 onion, chopped
2 garlic cloves, minced
2 teaspoons ground cumin
1 teaspoon ground coriander
1/2 teaspoon ground cinnamon
1/2 teaspoon ground turmeric
1/4 teaspoon cayenne pepper
2 cups dried red lentils, rinsed and drained
6 cups vegetable broth
1 can (14.5 oz) diced tomatoes, undrained
2 tablespoons tomato paste
1 lemon, juiced
Salt and pepper to taste
Chopped fresh cilantro, for garnish

Instructions:

In a large pot or Dutch oven, heat the olive oil over medium heat. Add the chopped onion and cook for 2-3 minutes, until softened.
Add the minced garlic, cumin, coriander, cinnamon, turmeric, and cayenne pepper to the pot. Cook for 1-2 minutes, stirring constantly, until fragrant.
Add the rinsed lentils, vegetable broth, diced tomatoes (with their juices), and tomato paste to the pot. Bring the mixture to a boil, then reduce the heat to low and simmer for 30-40 minutes, until the lentils are tender.
Remove the pot from the heat and use an immersion blender to puree the soup until smooth (alternatively, you can transfer the soup to a blender and blend in batches, then return to the pot).
Stir in the lemon juice and season the soup with salt and pepper to taste.
Serve the Moroccan Lentil Soup hot, garnished with chopped fresh cilantro.
Enjoy your delicious and nutritious Moroccan Lentil Soup!

Traditional Keftedes

Ingredients:

1 lb ground beef or lamb
1/2 cup breadcrumbs
1/4 cup grated onion
2 garlic cloves, minced
1/4 cup chopped fresh parsley
1/4 cup chopped fresh mint
1 egg, beaten
1 tablespoon ground cumin
1/2 teaspoon salt
1/4 teaspoon black pepper
Olive oil, for frying

Instructions:

In a large bowl, mix together the ground meat, breadcrumbs, grated onion, minced garlic, chopped parsley, chopped mint, beaten egg, ground cumin, salt, and black pepper until well combined.
Use your hands to shape the mixture into small meatballs, about 1-2 inches in diameter.
In a large skillet, heat enough olive oil to cover the bottom of the pan over medium heat. When the oil is hot, add the meatballs to the pan, being careful not to overcrowd them.
Fry the meatballs for 5-7 minutes per side, until browned and cooked through. Remove the meatballs from the skillet and drain on paper towels.
Serve the Traditional Keftedes hot, garnished with fresh parsley and mint.

Baked Keftedes

Ingredients:

1 lb ground beef or lamb
1/2 cup breadcrumbs
1/4 cup grated onion
2 garlic cloves, minced
1/4 cup chopped fresh parsley
1/4 cup chopped fresh mint
1 egg, beaten
1 tablespoon ground cumin
1/2 teaspoon salt
1/4 teaspoon black pepper
Olive oil spray

Instructions:

Preheat the oven to 375°F (190°C).
In a large bowl, mix together the ground meat, breadcrumbs, grated onion, minced garlic, chopped parsley, chopped mint, beaten egg, ground cumin, salt, and black pepper until well combined.
Use your hands to shape the mixture into small meatballs, about 1-2 inches in diameter.
Place the meatballs on a baking sheet lined with parchment paper.
Spray the meatballs lightly with olive oil spray.
Bake the meatballs in the preheated oven for 20-25 minutes, until browned and cooked through.
Serve the Baked Keftedes hot, garnished with fresh parsley and mint.
Enjoy your delicious and flavorful Keftedes!

Chicken Provençal

Ingredients:

4 bone-in, skin-on chicken thighs
Salt and black pepper, to taste
2 tablespoons olive oil
1 onion, chopped
4 garlic cloves, minced
1/2 cup chicken broth
1/2 cup dry white wine
1 can (14.5 oz) diced tomatoes, drained
1/4 cup chopped fresh parsley
2 tablespoons chopped fresh thyme
1 tablespoon chopped fresh rosemary
1/2 cup pitted Kalamata olives
1/4 cup capers, drained
Lemon wedges, for serving

Instructions:

Preheat the oven to 375°F (190°C).
Season the chicken thighs with salt and black pepper on both sides.
In a large skillet or Dutch oven, heat the olive oil over medium heat. When the oil is hot, add the chicken thighs to the pan, skin-side down. Cook for 5-7 minutes, until golden brown and crispy. Flip the chicken and cook for another 3-4 minutes on the other side. Remove the chicken from the skillet and set aside on a plate.
In the same skillet, add the chopped onion and minced garlic. Cook for 2-3 minutes, stirring constantly, until softened.
Pour the chicken broth and white wine into the skillet, scraping up any browned bits from the bottom of the pan. Add the diced tomatoes, chopped parsley, chopped thyme, and chopped rosemary to the pan. Stir to combine.
Return the chicken thighs to the skillet, skin-side up. Spoon the tomato mixture over the chicken.
Scatter the Kalamata olives and capers over the chicken and tomato mixture.
Cover the skillet with a lid or foil and transfer to the preheated oven. Bake for 30-35 minutes, until the chicken is cooked through and tender.
Serve the Chicken Provençal hot, garnished with lemon wedges.
Enjoy your delicious and fragrant Chicken Provençal!

Portuguese Mussels

Ingredients:

2 lbs fresh mussels, scrubbed and debearded
2 tablespoons olive oil
1 onion, chopped
4 garlic cloves, minced
1/2 cup dry white wine
1 can (14.5 oz) diced tomatoes, undrained
1 bay leaf
1/4 teaspoon red pepper flakes
1/4 cup chopped fresh parsley
Crusty bread, for serving

Instructions:
In a large pot or Dutch oven, heat the olive oil over medium heat. When the oil is hot, add the chopped onion and minced garlic. Cook for 2-3 minutes, stirring constantly, until softened.
Pour the white wine into the pot and bring to a boil. Add the diced tomatoes (with their juice), bay leaf, and red pepper flakes to the pot. Stir to combine.
Add the fresh mussels to the pot and cover with a lid. Cook for 5-7 minutes, shaking the pot occasionally, until the mussels have opened. Discard any mussels that have not opened.
Using a slotted spoon, transfer the cooked mussels to a serving dish. Pour the tomato and wine sauce over the mussels.
Sprinkle chopped fresh parsley over the mussels and sauce.
Serve the Portuguese Mussels hot, with crusty bread for soaking up the delicious sauce.
Enjoy your flavorful and aromatic Portuguese Mussels!

Soutzukakia

Soutzoukakia is a Greek meatball dish with Mediterranean spices. Here's a recipe to make it at home:

Ingredients:

1 lb ground beef
1/2 cup breadcrumbs
1 egg
1 onion, grated
2 garlic cloves, minced
1 tablespoon tomato paste
1 tablespoon red wine vinegar
1 tablespoon chopped fresh parsley
1 teaspoon ground cumin
1 teaspoon paprika
Salt and black pepper, to taste
Olive oil, for frying

For the Sauce:

1 can (14.5 oz) diced tomatoes
1 onion, chopped
2 garlic cloves, minced
1/2 cup chicken broth
1 tablespoon tomato paste
1 teaspoon dried oregano
Salt and black pepper, to taste

Instructions:

In a large mixing bowl, combine the ground beef, breadcrumbs, egg, grated onion, minced garlic, tomato paste, red wine vinegar, chopped parsley, ground cumin, paprika, salt, and black pepper. Mix well until all the ingredients are evenly combined.
Shape the mixture into oval-shaped meatballs, about 2 inches in length.
Heat the olive oil in a large skillet over medium heat. When the oil is hot, add the meatballs to the skillet and cook for 8-10 minutes, turning occasionally, until browned on all sides. Remove the meatballs from the skillet and set aside.
In the same skillet, add the chopped onion and minced garlic. Cook for 2-3 minutes, stirring constantly, until softened.
Pour the diced tomatoes (with their juice), chicken broth, tomato paste, dried oregano, salt, and black pepper into the skillet. Stir to combine.
Return the meatballs to the skillet and spoon the tomato sauce over them.
Reduce the heat to low and cover the skillet with a lid. Simmer for 20-25 minutes, until the meatballs are cooked through and tender.
Serve the Soutzoukakia hot, with the tomato sauce spooned over them. You can serve it with rice or crusty bread on the side.
Enjoy your delicious and fragrant Soutzoukakia!

Greek Chicken Souvlaki

Ingredients:

1 pound boneless, skinless chicken breasts, cut into cubes
1/4 cup olive oil
1/4 cup lemon juice
2 cloves garlic, minced
1 tablespoon dried oregano
1/2 teaspoon salt
1/4 teaspoon black pepper
1/4 teaspoon red pepper flakes (optional)
Wooden skewers
Tzatziki sauce for serving
Pita bread for serving
Sliced red onion, sliced tomato, and chopped parsley for garnish (optional)

Instructions:

In a bowl, whisk together the olive oil, lemon juice, garlic, oregano, salt, black pepper, and red pepper flakes (if using).
Add the chicken cubes to the marinade and stir to coat. Cover the bowl with plastic wrap and refrigerate for at least 30 minutes or up to 2 hours.
Preheat the grill to medium-high heat.
Thread the chicken cubes onto the wooden skewers, leaving a little space between each piece.
Grill the chicken skewers for 8 to 10 minutes, turning occasionally, until the chicken is cooked through and browned on all sides.
Remove the chicken skewers from the grill and let them rest for a few minutes.
Serve the chicken skewers with tzatziki sauce, pita bread, sliced red onion, sliced tomato, and chopped parsley (if using).
Enjoy your delicious Greek Chicken Souvlaki!

Mediterranean Zucchini Boats

Ingredients:

4 medium zucchinis
1/2 cup cooked quinoa
1/2 cup crumbled feta cheese
1/2 cup cherry tomatoes, halved
1/4 cup chopped kalamata olives
1/4 cup chopped fresh parsley
2 tablespoons olive oil
2 cloves garlic, minced
1/2 teaspoon dried oregano
Salt and black pepper, to taste
Lemon wedges, for serving (optional)

Instructions:

Preheat the oven to 400°F (200°C).
Cut the zucchinis in half lengthwise and scoop out the seeds with a spoon to create a hollow space in the center of each half. Place the zucchini halves in a baking dish.
In a bowl, combine the cooked quinoa, feta cheese, cherry tomatoes, kalamata olives, and parsley.
In a small saucepan, heat the olive oil over medium heat. Add the minced garlic and dried oregano and cook for 1 to 2 minutes, stirring constantly, until fragrant.
Pour the garlic and oregano mixture over the quinoa mixture and stir to combine. Season with salt and black pepper to taste.
Spoon the quinoa mixture into the hollowed-out zucchini halves, filling them generously.
Cover the baking dish with foil and bake for 25 to 30 minutes, or until the zucchinis are tender and the filling is hot and bubbly.
Remove from the oven and let cool for a few minutes before serving.
Serve the zucchini boats with lemon wedges on the side, if desired.
Enjoy your delicious Mediterranean Zucchini Boats!

Greek Moussaka

Ingredients:

2 large eggplants, sliced lengthwise
1 pound ground beef
1 onion, chopped
2 cloves garlic, minced
2 tablespoons tomato paste
1/2 cup red wine
1 can (14.5 oz) diced tomatoes
1 teaspoon dried oregano
1/4 teaspoon ground cinnamon
Salt and black pepper, to taste
3 tablespoons butter
3 tablespoons all-purpose flour
2 cups milk
1/4 teaspoon ground nutmeg
1/2 cup grated Parmesan cheese
1 egg, beaten

Instructions:

Preheat the oven to 375°F (190°C).
Arrange the eggplant slices on a baking sheet and brush both sides with olive oil. Bake for 20 to 25 minutes, or until tender and lightly browned. Set aside.
In a large skillet, cook the ground beef over medium heat until browned. Drain the excess fat.
Add the chopped onion and minced garlic to the skillet and cook until the onion is soft and translucent.
Stir in the tomato paste, red wine, diced tomatoes, oregano, cinnamon, salt, and black pepper. Bring to a simmer and cook for 10 to 15 minutes, or until the sauce is thick and flavorful.
In a small saucepan, melt the butter over medium heat. Whisk in the flour and cook for 1 to 2 minutes, stirring constantly, until the mixture is smooth and bubbly.
Gradually whisk in the milk and cook for 5 to 7 minutes, or until the sauce is thick and creamy.
Stir in the nutmeg and grated Parmesan cheese.
In a 9x13 inch baking dish, arrange half of the eggplant slices in a single layer. Spoon the meat sauce over the eggplant, spreading it evenly. Arrange the remaining eggplant slices on top of the meat sauce.
Whisk the beaten egg into the Parmesan cheese sauce and pour it over the top of the eggplant.
Bake for 30 to 35 minutes, or until the top is golden and the moussaka is hot and bubbly.
Let the moussaka cool for a few minutes before serving.
Enjoy your delicious Greek Moussaka!

Psari Plaki

Ingredients:

4 fillets of white fish (such as cod or halibut)
1 large onion, chopped
4 garlic cloves, minced
4 large ripe tomatoes, diced
1/4 cup chopped fresh parsley
1/4 cup chopped fresh dill
1/4 cup olive oil
1/4 cup white wine
Salt and black pepper, to taste
Lemon wedges, for serving (optional)

Instructions:

Preheat the oven to 375°F (190°C).
In a large baking dish, arrange the fish fillets in a single layer.
In a large skillet, heat the olive oil over medium heat. Add the chopped onion and minced garlic and cook for 3 to 5 minutes, or until the onion is soft and translucent.
Add the diced tomatoes, white wine, parsley, and dill to the skillet. Season with salt and black pepper to taste. Cook for 5 to 7 minutes, or until the sauce is thick and fragrant.
Spoon the tomato mixture over the fish fillets, spreading it evenly.
Cover the baking dish with foil and bake for 20 to 25 minutes, or until the fish is cooked through and flakes easily with a fork.
Remove the foil and bake for an additional 5 to 10 minutes, or until the top is lightly browned.
Let the psari plaki cool for a few minutes before serving.
Serve with lemon wedges on the side, if desired.
Enjoy your delicious Psari Plaki!

Mediterranean Chicken Skillet

Ingredients:

4 boneless, skinless chicken breasts
1 tablespoon olive oil
1 onion, chopped
3 cloves garlic, minced
1 red bell pepper, chopped
1 yellow bell pepper, chopped
1 zucchini, chopped
1 can (14.5 oz) diced tomatoes
1/2 cup pitted kalamata olives, chopped
1/4 cup chopped fresh parsley
1/4 cup chopped fresh basil
1 tablespoon capers
Salt and black pepper, to taste
Lemon wedges, for serving (optional)

Instructions:

Season the chicken breasts with salt and black pepper.
In a large skillet, heat the olive oil over medium-high heat. Add the chicken breasts and cook for 4 to 5 minutes per side, or until golden brown. Transfer the chicken to a plate and set aside.
In the same skillet, add the chopped onion and minced garlic. Cook for 3 to 4 minutes, or until the onion is soft and translucent.
Add the chopped red and yellow bell peppers and zucchini to the skillet. Cook for 5 to 7 minutes, or until the vegetables are tender.
Stir in the diced tomatoes, chopped kalamata olives, chopped parsley, chopped basil, and capers. Season with salt and black pepper to taste.
Nestle the chicken breasts in the skillet, spooning the vegetable mixture over the top of the chicken.
Cover the skillet with a lid and cook for 10 to 15 minutes, or until the chicken is cooked through and the vegetables are hot and bubbly.
Let the Mediterranean chicken skillet cool for a few minutes before serving. Serve with lemon wedges on the side, if desired.
Enjoy your delicious Mediterranean Chicken Skillet!

Pesto Bruschetta Chicken

Ingredients:

4 boneless, skinless chicken breasts
Salt and black pepper, to taste
1/2 cup prepared pesto
2 cups diced tomatoes
1/2 cup diced red onion
2 cloves garlic, minced
2 tablespoons balsamic vinegar
1 tablespoon olive oil
8 slices of baguette or Italian bread, toasted

Instructions:

Preheat the oven to 375°F (190°C).
Season the chicken breasts with salt and black pepper.
In a large skillet, heat the olive oil over medium-high heat. Add the chicken breasts and cook for 4 to 5 minutes per side, or until golden brown. Transfer the chicken to a baking dish and set aside.
Spread the prepared pesto over the chicken breasts.
In a medium bowl, mix together the diced tomatoes, red onion, minced garlic, balsamic vinegar, and a pinch of salt and black pepper.
Spoon the tomato mixture over the chicken breasts.
Bake for 20 to 25 minutes, or until the chicken is cooked through and the tomato mixture is hot and bubbly.
Top each slice of toasted bread with a chicken breast and some of the tomato mixture.
Serve the Pesto Bruschetta Chicken immediately.
Enjoy your delicious Pesto Bruschetta Chicken!

Loaded Layered Hummus Dip

Ingredients:

2 cups prepared hummus
1/2 cup diced cucumber
1/2 cup diced tomato
1/2 cup chopped kalamata olives
1/4 cup chopped fresh parsley
1/4 cup chopped fresh mint
1/4 cup crumbled feta cheese
1/4 cup chopped red onion
2 tablespoons olive oil
2 tablespoons lemon juice
Salt and black pepper, to taste
Pita chips or sliced vegetables, for serving

nstructions:

In a medium bowl, mix together the diced cucumber, diced tomato, chopped kalamata olives, chopped parsley, chopped mint, crumbled feta cheese, red onion, olive oil, lemon juice, salt, and black pepper.
Spread the prepared hummus in the bottom of a large serving dish.
Spoon the vegetable mixture over the hummus, spreading it out evenly.
Serve the Loaded Layered Hummus Dip with pita chips or sliced vegetables.

Enjoy your delicious Loaded Layered Hummus Dip!

Harissa Chicken

Ingredients:

4 boneless, skinless chicken breasts
Salt and black pepper, to taste
2 tablespoons harissa paste
2 tablespoons olive oil
1 lemon, juiced
4 garlic cloves, minced
1 teaspoon ground cumin
1 teaspoon ground coriander
1/2 teaspoon smoked paprika
1/2 teaspoon ground cinnamon
Lemon wedges, for serving (optional)

Instructions:

Preheat the oven to 375°F (190°C).
Season the chicken breasts with salt and black pepper.
In a medium bowl, mix together the harissa paste, olive oil, lemon juice, minced garlic, ground cumin, ground coriander, smoked paprika, and ground cinnamon.
Place the chicken breasts in a baking dish and spread the harissa mixture over the chicken, coating it evenly.
Bake for 20 to 25 minutes, or until the chicken is cooked through and no longer pink in the center.
Let the Harissa Chicken cool for a few minutes before serving.
Serve with lemon wedges on the side, if desired.
Enjoy your delicious and spicy Harissa Chicken!

Mediterranean Braised Chicken

Ingredients:

4 bone-in, skin-on chicken thighs
Salt and black pepper, to taste
2 tablespoons olive oil
1 large onion, chopped
4 garlic cloves, minced
1 red bell pepper, seeded and chopped
1 yellow bell pepper, seeded and chopped
1 teaspoon dried oregano
1 teaspoon dried thyme
1 teaspoon smoked paprika
1/2 teaspoon ground cinnamon
1/2 cup chicken broth
1/2 cup dry white wine
1/2 cup pitted kalamata olives
1/4 cup chopped fresh parsley
Lemon wedges, for serving (optional)

Instructions:

Preheat the oven to 375°F (190°C).
Season the chicken thighs with salt and black pepper.
In a large oven-safe skillet or Dutch oven, heat the olive oil over medium-high heat. Add the chicken thighs and cook for 4 to 5 minutes per side, or until golden brown. Transfer the chicken to a plate and set aside.
Add the chopped onion, minced garlic, chopped red and yellow bell peppers, dried oregano, dried thyme, smoked paprika, and ground cinnamon to the skillet. Cook for 5 to 7 minutes, or until the vegetables are tender.
Pour in the chicken broth and dry white wine, scraping the bottom of the skillet to release any browned bits. Bring to a simmer.
Return the chicken thighs to the skillet and spoon some of the vegetable mixture over the top of each thigh.
Cover the skillet or Dutch oven and transfer to the preheated oven. Bake for 30 to 35 minutes, or until the chicken is cooked through and the vegetables are soft and tender.
Remove the skillet from the oven and sprinkle the chopped kalamata olives and chopped fresh parsley over the top of the chicken and vegetables.
Serve the Mediterranean Braised Chicken with lemon wedges on the side, if desired.
Enjoy your delicious and rich Mediterranean Braised Chicken!

Mediterranean Stuffed Peppers

Ingredients:

4 bell peppers, any color
1 tablespoon olive oil
1 onion, chopped
3 garlic cloves, minced
1/2 cup diced tomatoes
1/2 cup cooked quinoa
1/2 cup cooked chickpeas
1/4 cup chopped fresh parsley
1/4 cup chopped fresh mint
1/4 cup crumbled feta cheese
2 tablespoons lemon juice
Salt and black pepper, to taste

Instructions:

Preheat the oven to 375°F (190°C).
Cut off the tops of the bell peppers and remove the seeds and membranes. Place the peppers in a baking dish.
In a large skillet, heat the olive oil over medium-high heat. Add the chopped onion and minced garlic and cook for 5 to 7 minutes, or until the onion is tender and translucent.
Add the diced tomatoes, cooked quinoa, cooked chickpeas, chopped parsley, chopped mint, crumbled feta cheese, lemon juice, salt, and black pepper to the skillet. Mix well.
Spoon the quinoa and chickpea mixture into the bell peppers, filling them to the top.
Cover the baking dish with aluminum foil and transfer to the preheated oven. Bake for 30 to 35 minutes, or until the peppers are tender and the filling is heated through.
Remove the baking dish from the oven and let the Mediterranean Stuffed Peppers cool for a few minutes before serving.
Enjoy your delicious and healthy Mediterranean Stuffed Peppers!

Ribollita (Tuscan White Bean Soup)

Ingredients:

1 large onion, chopped
3 garlic cloves, minced
2 celery stalks, chopped
2 carrots, chopped
1 can (14.5 oz) diced tomatoes
1 can (15 oz) cannellini beans, drained and rinsed
6 cups vegetable broth
2 cups chopped kale
2 cups chopped Swiss chard
2 cups cubed stale bread
1/4 cup grated Parmesan cheese
3 tablespoons olive oil
Salt and black pepper, to taste

Instructions:

In a large pot or Dutch oven, heat the olive oil over medium-high heat. Add the chopped onion and minced garlic and cook for 5 to 7 minutes, or until the onion is tender and translucent.
Add the chopped celery and chopped carrots and cook for another 5 to 7 minutes, or until the vegetables are slightly softened.
Add the diced tomatoes, drained and rinsed cannellini beans, and vegetable broth to the pot. Season with salt and black pepper to taste.
Bring the soup to a simmer and then reduce the heat to medium-low. Let the soup cook for 30 minutes.
Add the chopped kale, chopped Swiss chard, and cubed stale bread to the soup. Stir well to combine.
Cook the soup for another 10 to 15 minutes, or until the bread has softened and the kale and Swiss chard are tender.
Remove the pot from the heat and stir in the grated Parmesan cheese.
Serve the Ribollita hot, garnished with extra Parmesan cheese and a drizzle of olive oil.
Enjoy your delicious and hearty Ribollita Tuscan white bean soup!

Greek Steak Salad Bowl

Ingredients:

1 pound sirloin steak
1 teaspoon dried oregano
1/2 teaspoon garlic powder
1/2 teaspoon salt
1/4 teaspoon black pepper
4 cups chopped romaine lettuce
2 cups chopped cucumber
2 cups cherry tomatoes, halved
1/2 cup sliced red onion
1/2 cup crumbled feta cheese
1/4 cup pitted Kalamata olives
1/4 cup chopped fresh parsley
1/4 cup extra-virgin olive oil
2 tablespoons red wine vinegar
1 tablespoon lemon juice

Instructions:

Preheat the grill or grill pan to medium-high heat.
In a small bowl, mix together the dried oregano, garlic powder, salt, and black pepper. Rub the spice mixture all over the sirloin steak.
Grill the steak for 4 to 5 minutes per side, or until it reaches your desired level of doneness. Remove the steak from the grill and let it rest for 5 to 10 minutes before slicing it thinly.
In a large mixing bowl, combine the chopped romaine lettuce, chopped cucumber, halved cherry tomatoes, sliced red onion, crumbled feta cheese, pitted Kalamata olives, and chopped fresh parsley.
In a small bowl, whisk together the extra-virgin olive oil, red wine vinegar, and lemon juice. Pour the dressing over the salad and toss to coat.
Divide the salad mixture into bowls and top each bowl with sliced grilled steak. Serve the Greek Steak Salad Bowls immediately, garnished with extra feta cheese and parsley if desired.
Enjoy your delicious and healthy Greek Steak Salad Bowl!

Pipirrana

Ingredients:

2 large tomatoes, diced
1 green bell pepper, diced
1 red onion, diced
1/2 English cucumber, diced
2 hard-boiled eggs, chopped
1/4 cup extra-virgin olive oil
2 tablespoons red wine vinegar
1 teaspoon salt
1/4 teaspoon black pepper
1/4 cup chopped fresh parsley
1/4 cup chopped fresh mint

Instructions:

In a large mixing bowl, combine the diced tomatoes, diced green bell pepper, diced red onion, and diced cucumber.
Add the chopped hard-boiled eggs to the bowl and toss to combine.
In a small bowl, whisk together the extra-virgin olive oil, red wine vinegar, salt, and black pepper. Pour the dressing over the salad and toss to coat.
Add the chopped fresh parsley and chopped fresh mint to the salad and toss again.
Serve the Pipirrana chilled or at room temperature.
Enjoy your refreshing and flavorful Pipirrana salad!

Tortellini Pasta Salad

Ingredients:

1 pound cheese tortellini
1 cup cherry tomatoes, halved
1 cup diced cucumber
1 cup diced bell pepper (red, green, or yellow)
1/2 cup sliced black olives
1/4 cup diced red onion
1/4 cup chopped fresh basil
1/4 cup chopped fresh parsley
1/4 cup grated Parmesan cheese
1/4 cup extra-virgin olive oil
2 tablespoons red wine vinegar
2 cloves garlic, minced
1 teaspoon Dijon mustard
1/2 teaspoon salt
1/4 teaspoon black pepper

Instructions:

Cook the cheese tortellini according to the package instructions. Drain and rinse with cold water to stop the cooking process.
In a large mixing bowl, combine the cooked tortellini, cherry tomatoes, diced cucumber, diced bell pepper, sliced black olives, diced red onion, chopped fresh basil, chopped fresh parsley, and grated Parmesan cheese.
In a small bowl, whisk together the extra-virgin olive oil, red wine vinegar, minced garlic, Dijon mustard, salt, and black pepper. Pour the dressing over the pasta salad and toss to coat.
Chill the Tortellini Pasta Salad in the refrigerator for at least 30 minutes to allow the flavors to meld together.
Serve the Tortellini Pasta Salad cold, garnished with additional chopped fresh herbs and grated Parmesan cheese if desired.
Enjoy your delicious and easy-to-make Tortellini Pasta Salad!

Mediterranean Pasta

Ingredients:

1 pound dried penne pasta
1/2 cup extra-virgin olive oil
4 cloves garlic, minced
1/2 teaspoon red pepper flakes
1 cup cherry tomatoes, halved
1 cup pitted Kalamata olives, halved
1/2 cup chopped sun-dried tomatoes
1/4 cup chopped fresh parsley
1/4 cup chopped fresh basil
1/4 cup grated Parmesan cheese
Salt and black pepper, to taste

Instructions:

Cook the penne pasta in a large pot of salted boiling water according to the package instructions. Drain and set aside.
In a large skillet, heat the extra-virgin olive oil over medium heat. Add the minced garlic and red pepper flakes and cook for 1-2 minutes until fragrant.
Add the halved cherry tomatoes and cook for 5-7 minutes until softened and slightly caramelized.
Add the halved Kalamata olives and chopped sun-dried tomatoes to the skillet and cook for an additional 2-3 minutes.
Add the cooked penne pasta to the skillet and toss to combine with the tomato and olive mixture.
Stir in the chopped fresh parsley, chopped fresh basil, and grated Parmesan cheese. Season with salt and black pepper to taste.
Serve the Mediterranean Pasta hot, garnished with additional grated Parmesan cheese and chopped fresh herbs if desired.
Enjoy your delicious and flavorful Mediterranean Pasta!

Batata Harra

Ingredients:

1 1/2 pounds potatoes, peeled and diced into small cubes
1/4 cup extra-virgin olive oil
4 cloves garlic, minced
1/2 teaspoon cayenne pepper
1/2 teaspoon paprika
1/2 teaspoon ground cumin
1/2 teaspoon salt
1/4 teaspoon black pepper
1/4 cup chopped fresh cilantro
Juice of 1 lemon

Instructions:

In a large skillet, heat the extra-virgin olive oil over medium-high heat. Add the diced potatoes and cook for 10-12 minutes, stirring occasionally, until golden and crispy on the outside and tender on the inside.
Add the minced garlic, cayenne pepper, paprika, ground cumin, salt, and black pepper to the skillet and cook for an additional 1-2 minutes until fragrant.
Remove the skillet from the heat and stir in the chopped fresh cilantro and lemon juice.
Serve the Batata Harra hot as a side dish or snack.
Enjoy your delicious and spicy Batata Harra!

Cherry Tomato Gratin

Ingredients:

2 cups cherry tomatoes, halved
1/2 cup grated Parmesan cheese
1/2 cup panko breadcrumbs
1/4 cup chopped fresh basil
2 tablespoons extra-virgin olive oil
2 cloves garlic, minced
Salt and black pepper, to taste

Instructions:

Preheat your oven to 400°F (200°C).
In a large mixing bowl, combine the halved cherry tomatoes, grated Parmesan cheese, panko breadcrumbs, and chopped fresh basil.
In a separate small mixing bowl, whisk together the extra-virgin olive oil and minced garlic until well combined.
Drizzle the garlic and oil mixture over the cherry tomato mixture and toss to combine.
Season the mixture with salt and black pepper to taste.
Pour the tomato mixture into a 9-inch baking dish and spread it out into an even layer.
Bake the Cherry Tomato Gratin in the preheated oven for 15-20 minutes until the top is golden brown and crispy.
Remove the baking dish from the oven and allow it to cool for a few minutes before serving.
Enjoy your delicious and savory Cherry Tomato Gratin!

Israeli Couscous Salad

Ingredients:

1 1/2 cups Israeli couscous
2 cups water
1/2 teaspoon salt
1 red bell pepper, diced
1 yellow bell pepper, diced
1/2 cup cherry tomatoes, halved
1/4 cup chopped fresh parsley
1/4 cup chopped fresh mint
1/4 cup chopped fresh basil
1/4 cup crumbled feta cheese
1/4 cup extra-virgin olive oil
2 tablespoons freshly squeezed lemon juice
1 teaspoon honey
Salt and black pepper, to taste

Instructions:

In a medium-sized saucepan, bring the water to a boil. Add the Israeli couscous and 1/2 teaspoon salt and reduce the heat to low. Cover the saucepan and simmer for 10-12 minutes until the couscous is tender and the water is absorbed.
Remove the couscous from the heat and fluff it with a fork. Set it aside to cool.
In a large mixing bowl, combine the cooled couscous, diced red and yellow bell peppers, halved cherry tomatoes, chopped fresh parsley, mint, and basil, and crumbled feta cheese.
In a separate small mixing bowl, whisk together the extra-virgin olive oil, freshly squeezed lemon juice, honey, salt, and black pepper until well combined.
Pour the dressing over the couscous mixture and toss everything together until the salad is well coated.
Serve the Israeli Couscous Salad chilled or at room temperature.
Enjoy your delicious and colorful Israeli Couscous Salad!

Pesto Sauce

Here's a recipe for a classic basil pesto sauce:

Ingredients:

2 cups fresh basil leaves, packed
1/2 cup freshly grated Parmesan cheese
1/2 cup extra-virgin olive oil
1/3 cup pine nuts (or walnuts)
3 garlic cloves, minced
Salt and freshly ground black pepper, to taste

Instructions:

In a food processor or blender, combine the basil leaves, Parmesan cheese, pine nuts, garlic, salt, and black pepper.
Pulse the mixture until it is coarsely chopped.
While the food processor is running, slowly pour in the olive oil until the mixture is well blended and smooth.
Taste the pesto sauce and adjust the seasoning if necessary, adding more salt or pepper as desired.
Transfer the pesto sauce to a jar or container with a tight-fitting lid and store it in the refrigerator until ready to use.
Note: Pesto sauce can also be made with different variations such as using different herbs like cilantro or parsley, using different nuts like almonds or cashews, or adding lemon juice or chili flakes for added flavor.

North African Chermoula

Ingredients:

2 bunches fresh parsley, chopped
1 bunch fresh cilantro, chopped
1/2 cup extra-virgin olive oil
1/4 cup freshly squeezed lemon juice
4 garlic cloves, minced
2 teaspoons paprika
2 teaspoons ground cumin
1 teaspoon ground coriander
1/2 teaspoon ground cinnamon
Salt and freshly ground black pepper, to taste

Instructions:

In a medium-sized mixing bowl, combine the chopped parsley and cilantro, minced garlic, paprika, cumin, coriander, cinnamon, salt, and black pepper.
Stir in the olive oil and lemon juice until the mixture is well combined.
Transfer the chermoula to a jar or container with a tight-fitting lid and store it in the refrigerator for at least 30 minutes to allow the flavors to meld together.
Use the chermoula as a marinade for fish, chicken, or vegetables before grilling, roasting, or baking. It can also be used as a sauce for dipping or as a condiment for sandwiches or salads. Enjoy!

Mediterranean Quinoa Salad

Ingredients:

1 cup quinoa
2 cups water
1 cup cherry tomatoes, halved
1 cucumber, diced
1 red onion, diced
1 red bell pepper, diced
1/2 cup Kalamata olives, pitted and chopped
1/2 cup crumbled feta cheese
1/4 cup chopped fresh parsley
1/4 cup chopped fresh mint
1/4 cup extra-virgin olive oil
2 tablespoons freshly squeezed lemon juice
Salt and freshly ground black pepper, to taste

Instructions:

Rinse the quinoa in a fine-mesh strainer and place it in a medium-sized saucepan. Add the water and a pinch of salt and bring to a boil over medium-high heat.
Reduce the heat to low, cover the saucepan, and simmer the quinoa for 15-20 minutes, or until the water has been absorbed and the quinoa is tender.
Remove the saucepan from the heat and let it sit for 5 minutes before fluffing the quinoa with a fork.
Transfer the quinoa to a large mixing bowl and add the cherry tomatoes, cucumber, red onion, red bell pepper, Kalamata olives, feta cheese, parsley, and mint.
In a small mixing bowl, whisk together the olive oil, lemon juice, salt, and black pepper.
Pour the dressing over the quinoa salad and toss to combine.
Serve the salad chilled or at room temperature. Enjoy!

Moroccan Couscous

Ingredients:

1 1/2 cups couscous
2 cups vegetable broth
2 tablespoons olive oil
1 onion, chopped
3 garlic cloves, minced
1 teaspoon ground cumin
1 teaspoon ground coriander
1/2 teaspoon ground cinnamon
1/4 teaspoon ground turmeric
1/4 teaspoon cayenne pepper
Salt and freshly ground black pepper, to taste
1/2 cup raisins
1/2 cup sliced almonds, toasted
1/2 cup chopped fresh parsley
1/4 cup chopped fresh cilantro

Instructions:

In a medium-sized saucepan, bring the vegetable broth to a boil. Stir in the couscous, cover the saucepan, and remove it from the heat. Let it sit for 10 minutes to allow the couscous to absorb the liquid.
In a large skillet, heat the olive oil over medium heat. Add the onion and garlic and sauté for 5-7 minutes, or until the onion is softened.
Stir in the cumin, coriander, cinnamon, turmeric, cayenne pepper, salt, and black pepper, and sauté for another 2-3 minutes.
Fluff the couscous with a fork and transfer it to the skillet with the onion mixture.
Add the raisins, toasted almonds, parsley, and cilantro to the skillet and stir to combine.
Cook the couscous mixture over low heat for 5-10 minutes, or until heated through and the flavors have melded together.
Serve the Moroccan couscous as a side dish or as a main dish with additional vegetables or protein if desired. Enjoy!

Sicilian Pasta

Ingredients:

1 pound spaghetti
1/2 cup olive oil
1/2 cup breadcrumbs
3 garlic cloves, minced
1/2 teaspoon red pepper flakes
1/2 cup raisins
1/2 cup pine nuts
1/2 cup chopped fresh parsley
Salt and freshly ground black pepper, to taste
Grated Parmesan cheese, for serving

Instructions:

Cook the spaghetti in a large pot of salted boiling water according to package directions until al dente. Reserve 1/2 cup of the pasta cooking water before draining.
While the pasta cooks, heat the olive oil in a large skillet over medium heat. Add the breadcrumbs and stir to coat with the oil. Cook, stirring frequently, for 3-4 minutes or until the breadcrumbs are golden brown and crispy.
Add the garlic and red pepper flakes to the skillet and sauté for 1-2 minutes, or until fragrant.
Stir in the raisins, pine nuts, and parsley, and season with salt and black pepper.
Add the cooked spaghetti to the skillet and toss to combine with the breadcrumb mixture. If the pasta seems dry, add some of the reserved pasta cooking water to loosen it up.
Serve the Sicilian pasta hot, topped with grated Parmesan cheese. Enjoy!

Green Beans Almondine

Ingredients:

1 pound green beans, trimmed
2 tablespoons unsalted butter
1/4 cup sliced almonds
2 garlic cloves, minced
1 tablespoon lemon juice
Salt and freshly ground black pepper, to taste

Instructions:

Bring a large pot of salted water to a boil. Add the green beans and cook for 3-4 minutes, or until they are tender-crisp.
Drain the green beans and immediately transfer them to a bowl of ice water to stop the cooking process. Drain again and pat dry with paper towels.
Melt the butter in a large skillet over medium heat. Add the sliced almonds and sauté for 2-3 minutes, or until they are lightly golden brown.
Add the garlic to the skillet and sauté for 1-2 minutes, or until fragrant.
Add the green beans to the skillet and toss to coat with the almond-garlic butter. Drizzle the lemon juice over the top and season with salt and black pepper to taste.
Cook the green beans for another 2-3 minutes, or until they are heated through and the flavors have melded together.
Transfer the green beans almondine to a serving dish and sprinkle with additional sliced almonds if desired. Serve hot and enjoy!

Ham and Swiss Quiche

Ingredients:

1 unbaked 9-inch pie crust
1 cup cooked ham, chopped
1 cup shredded Swiss cheese
4 large eggs
1 cup heavy cream
1/2 cup milk
1/4 teaspoon salt
1/4 teaspoon black pepper
1/4 teaspoon paprika
2 tablespoons chopped fresh parsley

Instructions:

Preheat the oven to 375°F (190°C).
Place the pie crust in a 9-inch pie dish and crimp the edges as desired.
Spread the chopped ham evenly over the bottom of the pie crust, then sprinkle the shredded Swiss cheese over the top.
In a large mixing bowl, whisk together the eggs, heavy cream, milk, salt, black pepper, and paprika until well combined.
Pour the egg mixture over the ham and cheese in the pie crust.
Bake the quiche for 35-40 minutes, or until the filling is set and the top is lightly golden brown.
Remove the quiche from the oven and let it cool for 5-10 minutes before slicing and serving.
Sprinkle chopped fresh parsley over the top of the quiche before serving, if desired. Enjoy!

Avgolemono Soup

Ingredients:

8 cups chicken broth
1 cup long-grain white rice
3 large eggs
1/2 cup freshly squeezed lemon juice
Salt and freshly ground black pepper, to taste
Chopped fresh parsley or dill, for garnish

Instructions:

In a large pot, bring the chicken broth to a boil over high heat.
Add the rice to the pot and reduce the heat to medium-low. Simmer the rice for 15-20 minutes, or until tender.
In a mixing bowl, whisk together the eggs and lemon juice until well combined.
Once the rice is cooked, remove the pot from the heat and ladle about 1 cup of the hot broth into the egg-lemon mixture while whisking constantly.
Gradually add another 2 cups of the hot broth to the egg-lemon mixture while continuing to whisk vigorously.
Pour the egg-lemon mixture back into the pot with the remaining broth and rice, whisking constantly to combine.
Return the pot to medium heat and cook the soup for 5-7 minutes, or until the broth has thickened slightly and the soup is hot.
Season the soup with salt and black pepper to taste.
Serve the avgolemono soup hot, garnished with chopped fresh parsley or dill.
Enjoy!

Mediterranean Omelette

Ingredients:

3 large eggs
1 tablespoon olive oil
1/4 cup chopped red onion
1/4 cup chopped bell pepper
1/4 cup chopped tomatoes
1/4 cup crumbled feta cheese
1 tablespoon chopped fresh parsley
Salt and freshly ground black pepper, to taste

Instructions:

In a mixing bowl, whisk the eggs until well beaten.
Heat the olive oil in a nonstick skillet over medium-high heat.
Add the chopped red onion and bell pepper to the skillet and sauté for 2-3 minutes, or until the vegetables are tender.
Add the chopped tomatoes to the skillet and cook for another 1-2 minutes, or until the tomatoes are slightly softened.
Pour the beaten eggs into the skillet with the vegetables and stir gently with a spatula to distribute the vegetables evenly.
Cook the omelette for 2-3 minutes, or until the bottom is lightly browned and the top is set.
Sprinkle the crumbled feta cheese and chopped fresh parsley over one half of the omelette.
Use the spatula to fold the other half of the omelette over the cheese and herbs.
Cook the omelette for an additional 1-2 minutes, or until the cheese is melted and the eggs are fully cooked.
Season the omelette with salt and black pepper to taste.
Slide the omelette onto a plate and serve hot. Enjoy!

Mediterranean fish gratins

Ingredients:

1 lb white fish fillets (such as cod or haddock)
Salt and freshly ground black pepper, to taste
2 tablespoons olive oil
1 small onion, chopped
2 garlic cloves, minced
1 red bell pepper, chopped
1/4 cup white wine
1 (14.5 oz) can diced tomatoes
1 teaspoon dried oregano
1/2 teaspoon paprika
1/4 teaspoon cayenne pepper (optional)
1/2 cup panko breadcrumbs
1/4 cup grated Parmesan cheese
2 tablespoons chopped fresh parsley

Instructions:

Preheat the oven to 375°F.
Season the fish fillets with salt and black pepper on both sides.
Heat the olive oil in a large skillet over medium heat.
Add the chopped onion and garlic to the skillet and sauté for 2-3 minutes, or until the onion is translucent.
Add the chopped red bell pepper to the skillet and sauté for another 2-3 minutes, or until the pepper is tender.
Pour the white wine into the skillet and bring to a simmer.
Add the diced tomatoes, dried oregano, paprika, and cayenne pepper (if using) to the skillet and stir to combine.
Simmer the tomato sauce for 5-7 minutes, or until slightly thickened.
Arrange the seasoned fish fillets in a single layer in a large baking dish.
Spoon the tomato sauce over the fish fillets, making sure to cover them completely.
In a small mixing bowl, combine the panko breadcrumbs, grated Parmesan cheese, and chopped fresh parsley.
Sprinkle the breadcrumb mixture evenly over the top of the fish and tomato sauce.
Bake the fish gratin in the preheated oven for 20-25 minutes, or until the fish is cooked through and the breadcrumb topping is golden brown.
Remove the fish gratin from the oven and let it rest for a few minutes before serving. Enjoy!

Speedy Mediterranean gnocchi

Ingredients:

1 lb package of gnocchi
2 tablespoons olive oil
1 small onion, chopped
2 cloves garlic, minced
1 red bell pepper, chopped
1 small zucchini, chopped
1 cup cherry tomatoes, halved
1/4 cup Kalamata olives, pitted and halved
1/4 cup crumbled feta cheese
2 tablespoons chopped fresh parsley
Salt and freshly ground black pepper, to taste

Instructions:

Cook the gnocchi according to package instructions until al dente. Drain and set aside.
Heat the olive oil in a large skillet over medium heat.
Add the chopped onion and minced garlic to the skillet and sauté for 2-3 minutes, or until the onion is translucent.
Add the chopped red bell pepper and zucchini to the skillet and sauté for another 2-3 minutes, or until the vegetables are tender.
Add the halved cherry tomatoes and Kalamata olives to the skillet and stir to combine.
Season the vegetable mixture with salt and black pepper to taste.
Add the cooked gnocchi to the skillet and stir to combine with the vegetable mixture.
Cook the gnocchi and vegetables for 2-3 minutes, or until heated through.
Sprinkle the crumbled feta cheese over the top of the gnocchi and vegetables.
Garnish with chopped fresh parsley before serving. Enjoy!

Mediterranean spelt-stuffed peppers

Ingredients:

4 bell peppers, tops cut off and seeds removed
1 cup spelt berries
2 cups vegetable broth
1 tablespoon olive oil
1 small onion, chopped
2 cloves garlic, minced
1 small zucchini, diced
1/2 cup chopped sun-dried tomatoes
1/4 cup chopped Kalamata olives
1/4 cup crumbled feta cheese
2 tablespoons chopped fresh parsley
Salt and freshly ground black pepper, to taste

Instructions:

Preheat the oven to 375°F.
Rinse the spelt berries and add them to a medium saucepan with the vegetable broth. Bring the mixture to a boil over high heat, then reduce the heat to low and simmer for 25-30 minutes, or until the spelt is tender and the broth has been absorbed.
While the spelt is cooking, heat the olive oil in a large skillet over medium heat.
Add the chopped onion and minced garlic to the skillet and sauté for 2-3 minutes, or until the onion is translucent.
Add the diced zucchini to the skillet and sauté for another 2-3 minutes, or until the zucchini is tender.
Add the chopped sun-dried tomatoes and Kalamata olives to the skillet and stir to combine.
Season the vegetable mixture with salt and black pepper to taste.
Add the cooked spelt to the skillet and stir to combine with the vegetable mixture.
Spoon the spelt and vegetable mixture into the prepared bell peppers, filling them to the top.
Place the stuffed peppers in a baking dish and bake for 25-30 minutes, or until the peppers are tender and the filling is heated through.
Sprinkle the crumbled feta cheese over the top of the stuffed peppers.
Garnish with chopped fresh parsley before serving. Enjoy!

Slow-cooker Spanish chicken

Ingredients:

1 1/2 lbs. boneless, skinless chicken breasts or thighs, cut into bite-sized pieces
1 red onion, sliced
1 red bell pepper, sliced
1 green bell pepper, sliced
4 garlic cloves, minced
1 teaspoon smoked paprika
1 teaspoon dried oregano
1 teaspoon ground cumin
1/2 teaspoon salt
1/4 teaspoon black pepper
1/4 cup chicken broth
1/4 cup dry white wine
1 (14.5 oz.) can diced tomatoes, undrained
1/4 cup chopped fresh parsley, for garnish
Cooked rice, for serving

Instructions:

In a slow cooker, combine the chicken, sliced red onion, sliced red and green bell peppers, minced garlic, smoked paprika, dried oregano, ground cumin, salt, and black pepper. Stir to combine.
Add the chicken broth, dry white wine, and diced tomatoes with their juices to the slow cooker. Stir to combine.
Cover the slow cooker and cook on low for 6-8 hours, or until the chicken is tender and cooked through.
Serve the Spanish chicken over cooked rice, garnished with chopped fresh parsley. Enjoy!

Spanish meatball & butter bean stew

Ingredients:

500g beef mince
1 onion, finely chopped
2 garlic cloves, minced
2 tbsp breadcrumbs
1 egg, lightly beaten
1 tsp smoked paprika
Salt and pepper
2 tbsp olive oil
2 cans of butter beans, drained and rinsed
1 can of chopped tomatoes
2 cups of beef stock
1 red bell pepper, sliced
1 green bell pepper, sliced
1 tsp dried oregano

Instructions:

In a large mixing bowl, combine the beef mince, onion, garlic, breadcrumbs, egg, smoked paprika, salt and pepper. Mix well until all the ingredients are fully incorporated.
Form the mixture into small meatballs, roughly the size of a golf ball.
Heat the olive oil in a large frying pan over medium heat. Add the meatballs and cook for 8-10 minutes, turning frequently until browned on all sides.
Remove the meatballs from the pan and set them aside.
Add the sliced peppers to the same frying pan and cook for 2-3 minutes until softened.
Add the chopped tomatoes, beef stock and oregano to the pan and stir to combine.
Return the meatballs to the pan, along with the drained and rinsed butter beans. Stir gently to combine.
Bring the mixture to a simmer, then reduce the heat to low and cover the pan. Cook for 30-35 minutes, stirring occasionally, until the meatballs are fully cooked and the stew has thickened.
Season with salt and pepper to taste.
Serve the Spanish meatball and butter bean stew hot, garnished with fresh parsley or chopped coriander. Enjoy!

Caponata

Ingredients:

1 large eggplant, diced
1 onion, diced
2 garlic cloves, minced
1 red bell pepper, diced
1 yellow bell pepper, diced
1/4 cup olive oil
1/4 cup red wine vinegar
1 can of chopped tomatoes
2 tbsp tomato paste
2 tbsp capers, drained and rinsed
1/2 cup pitted green olives, sliced
2 tbsp sugar
Salt and pepper
Fresh parsley, chopped for garnish

Instructions:

Heat the olive oil in a large frying pan over medium heat. Add the diced eggplant and cook until golden brown and softened, about 10-12 minutes. Remove from the pan and set aside.
In the same pan, add the onion and garlic and sauté until softened, about 5 minutes.
Add the diced red and yellow bell peppers to the pan and sauté for another 5 minutes.
Add the can of chopped tomatoes and tomato paste to the pan and stir to combine.
Simmer for 10-15 minutes, or until the vegetables are cooked through and the sauce has thickened.
Add the cooked eggplant, capers, olives, red wine vinegar, sugar, salt and pepper to the pan. Stir gently to combine.
Simmer for another 10-15 minutes, stirring occasionally, until the flavors have melded together.
Adjust seasoning to taste with salt and pepper.
Remove from heat and let cool to room temperature.
Serve the caponata at room temperature, garnished with chopped fresh parsley. It can be served as a side dish or appetizer, and is often eaten with crusty bread. Enjoy!

I want to take a moment to express my heartfelt gratitude for your recent purchase of my recipe book. As a passionate food lover, nothing makes me happier than sharing my favorite recipes with others. Your decision to invest in my book not only supports my dream, but also shows your commitment to expanding your culinary horizons.

I sincerely hope that the recipes in the book will inspire you to try new things and add some excitement to your meals.

Thank you again for your support and for being a part of this journey with me. I hope my book will bring you many happy and delicious moments in the kitchen.

www.ingramcontent.com/pod-product-compliance
Lightning Source LLC
Chambersburg PA
CBHW042121100526
44587CB00025B/4146